To Nadia

2

A Letter To My Daughter

by

Nina Simone Gaines

Table of Contents

1. Birth of a Child

2. Love

3. Positive Thinking

4. Inner Power

5. Giving

6. Laughter

7. The Journey

8. Health

9. Travel

10.   Unplug

11.   True Purpose for Money

12.   Inner Beauty

13.   Children are Gifts

My Dearest Daughter,

I want to start off by telling you how much I love you and that you are the Best Blessing that ever came into my life. I remember the first time I saw you, no hair, so chubby (8.5 pounds), quiet. You did not cry until the nurses started cleaning you off. They wrapped you up and handed you to me. Wow, I was a Mom! I could not believe that you came out of me. I just stared at you, who then immediately let me know that it was time to eat (You still have a hearty appetite). I remember trying to get you to latch on, but you seemed to want a quicker way to get fed. I think back on how painful it felt but, was determined to help you adjust to your new way of eating. I am so grateful for patience. You were such a delightful child, funny, always happy and smiling. You were obedient, so smart and a mother's joy. I remember one night when I was pregnant, not sure of the month, but I could not sleep and as usual was watching infomercials. I saw an infomercial for Hooked on Phonics. I remember my collection of Phonics workbooks and just knew that I had to get you a set. I taught you how to read at the age of three. *Do you remember how*

I use to make you sit at the kitchen table and make you repeat cat, sat, hat, rat, bat? I still laugh at your stubbornness and frowns. You just wanted to go outside and play. Now look at you all grown up. I will never forget when I signed you up to take the SAT in the seventh grade and you scored 1350 out of 2400. I knew in that moment that I had made the right decision to buy Hooked on Phonics and also buying all of those Disney Books instead of movies. I think you were 15 when you realized that out of all of your friends, you were the only one who had not seen all of the popular Disney movies but had instead read the books. I laugh as I remember you saying

"Mom, REALLY how come I have not seen Beauty and the Beast?" I pray that you always keep your love for reading and instill it in your children and help to mentor the next generation. (I thank my Mother).

My Dearest Daughter,

You were nine years old when your dad and I got divorced. You screamed a scream that pierced through my soul.

My heart broke knowing that we caused you so much pain. I think we both tried to overcompensate with material things to help ease your pain and our conscious (although I cannot speak for your father), but when your whole world as you know it gets turned upside down no material object will do. I am so sorry that you had to experience such pain. I pray that you know nothing you did or didn't do caused the divorce. I want you to know that your parents were in love. I want you to remember that when you fall in love, it is a beautiful feeling. It is like having your breath taken away as soon as you see that person. Or like, having a warmth come over you, a tingling feeling inside the pit of your stomach. Oh my dearest daughter, when you fall in love, you feel inspired to conquer the world. You feel as though everything in life is moving for your benefit. You find yourself smiling for no reason, giggling inside as though only the two of you share this special feeling. Falling in love makes you feel young, light on your feet, in the mood to give out hugs to everyone. My dearest daughter when you fall in love, you will know. It will be like something you just cannot explain. You will know that he is the right one for you. Do you remember the first time that guy told you he loved you and I said he was just saying it to "push" the relationship forward? Do you remember when you found out that he was very "popular" with the girls? I know you are glad that you listened to your Mom. I pray that you wait for the right person to fall in love with. It is a beautiful thing and deserves the utmost respect. If a guy truly loves you, he will not only say it but show you in the most sweet, sincere and heartfelt ways. Love is kind and patient. Love does not bring you harm or pain. Love has your back when it seems like the whole world is against you. Love will inspire you and love you unconditionally. Love is free and would never ask you to compromise your body or beliefs for any type of immediate gratification. Love is the power within that encompasses all that is beautiful. (I am grateful to have been in love).

My Dearest Daughter,

Do you remember when you would become worried, anxious and overwhelmed in school-usually the first semester? Do you remember when I would say "everything will be okay, it's all going to work out just change your thinking." Always think positive towards everything in life. Even when a bad situation occurs, find the good in it. Positive thinking will help you when you are sad, sick, hurt, have any type of lack (money, relationship etc.) in life. Once you start thinking positive, you can't help but start feeling good and might even crack a smile. You must know that positive thinking will keep you stress free, relaxed, and helps maintain a happiness within that is so essential for your well-being. Positive thinking will give you peace of mind when everything around you seems to be falling apart. "Everything will be okay."

(I love you)

My Dearest Daughter,

There is a power inside of you that dwells in all of us. This power is often not found or sought by most people. I want you to know that because you have this power inside of you, everything is possible, there is no lack, weakness, sadness, no darkness or misery. This power inside of you encompasses everlasting light, all knowledge, all resources, all strength, all love, all courage, all harmony and happiness. This power is in you. I pray that you tap into it whenever you have a need or want for anything in life. This power will guide and protect you keeping you safe from all harm. Just ask and you shall receive whatever it is that you need in order to live more, do more and be more in life. Believe it with all of your heart no matter what your surrounding environment may look like, BELIEVE.

My Dearest Daughter,

Giving comes in so many forms. Do you remember when we lived in that little one bedroom apartment? It was in that apartment that I learned about true charity. I learned that even if you do not have money, you can give a smile to a stranger, or speak kind words to someone. You can give a hug (I tried to give you as many as I could daily) to a loved one or friend. You can sit with an elderly neighbor/friend or call up someone to let them know that you were thinking of them. I learned that when you do get some money, give to a worthy cause or to someone in need.

Even though, I did not have a steady stream of income, I gave more in charity than I ever did when I worked at a 9 to 5 job. My dearest daughter, do not let a day go by where you have not given a kind word, gesture, act or dollar to someone else in need. Sometimes you can sense someone's sadness which would be a good time to give. Remember to give without seeking praise or acknowledgment. Give more than you take in life.

My Dearest Daughter,

Remember to always laugh. Do you remember how much laughter we have shared? Never take yourself or life so serious. Laughter makes you feel good; helps you to remember that life is meant to be enjoyed even with laughter. Do you remember how we would find something so funny that we would actually start crying? I'm laughing now just thinking about it. Do you remember when we lived in that one bedroom apartment? We laughed more in that little space than we did in all of the houses, apartments and condos we ever lived in. We had less in that space, ,including no car, but laughed more, dreamed more, grew more in spirit than ever. My dearest daughter always remember that it does not matter where you live or where you come from, happiness and laughter come from within. (Look inside and tap into your power).

My Dearest Daughter,

Learn to appreciate the journey. The journey is where all the magic/good times happen. On the journey, your creativity will grow, you will mature, and realize your strength. No matter what you do, never give up when you make up your mind to do something. Do not be afraid to think BIG! Remember EVERYTHING is Possible. My dearest daughter, when you think Big, you might realize that you have become separate from others that were once a regular presence. It takes a lot of courage, determination, desire and unwavering faith to think Big. You have to know that your journey will be extraordinary. Remember mediocrity is not an option, ever. Remember to enjoy the journey and know that you will reach your goals. Do you remember when I would kiss you goodbye on your way to school and would say "Make good choices"? On your journey make good choices and even if you make some bad ones, remember to find the good in the bad choice. Also do not give in to fear if your journey should set forth on a different path. There are many paths in life to choose from, it's up to you and you alone to decide which path is right for you. If you ever feel like you have lost your way, remember to look inside, quiet yourself, your environment and listen for the voice inside. You are destined for Greatness.

My Dearest Daughter,

Do you remember our weekend runs/walks? I loved those times. I remember feeling terrible one day, but you had your heart set on running. I never told you that I was in in so much pain that I could barely walk but I wanted you to get your miles in that day. My daughter, exercise is so important. Whether you run, walk, skip, jump, swim, (Just Dance), you have to keep moving. When you stay healthy you decrease so many potential occurrences for illnesses. You know that I have never been strict with your eating habits (gave you ice cream if you craved it even for breakfast sometimes) but I always made sure that you were in shape, healthy never over doing it. I just wanted you to make healthy choices, providing you with some kind of vegetable with your dinners-balance. Do you remember when I tricked you into eating spinach by putting cheese on it?

You would not eat the spinach, so I added cheese the next time I cooked it without telling you that it was spinach. (So funny). I am grateful that you are healthy, and eat all kinds of vegetables now. Remember to have balance my dearest daughter. You can enjoy all types of foods, just as long as you keep a balance (Burn more than you take in is key). And NEVER forget, the importance of water.

My Dearest Daughter,

See the world! Travel as often as you can. I remember getting your first passport when you were in the 7th grade because I wanted to show you the world. I wanted you to experience other cultures, their food, and to see people of all different races, shapes, backgrounds, languages. I wanted you to gain a global way of thinking, learning that we are all One Humanity. I wanted to show you how our one bedroom apartment would seem like a mansion to someone who had to build their house from clay or cow dung. I wanted to travel with you and show you how children in other parts of the world would love to have just one pair of the many shoes that you had in your closet.(I hope you understand why I always gave our unused items to Goodwill). My dearest daughter I want you to travel and see the world as it really is and not how it appears on television. Travel as much as you can. I pray that in your travels you experience humility and appreciation for the simplest things such as indoor plumbing or clean water and learn the importance of loving all mankind and wanting for others what you want for yourself.

My Dearest Daughter,

Remember to unplug. I am not sure how advanced technology will go, but I do know that it will be very important for you to learn how to unplug. Periodically, unplug from your phone, the internet, cable television, radio, social media etc. Learn to be comfortable in silence which by the way is when you will be able to hear your inner voice. Learn to quiet yourself, hear the silence, or the birds chirping, the ocean waves, the wind blowing, nature. Learn to appreciate nature's beauty, its colors and how pleasant you feel in its presence.

Remember that it is essential for your well-being, spirit and peace of mind to unplug from time to time. I promise you that you will always have a sense of newness, and refreshed being when you unplug.

My Dearest Daughter,

Money is for Service. Money enables you to do more, have more, live more freely. But understand, it is not for excess.

You can use money to buy nice things, live in a nice house/condo, travel etc. (you deserve the very best-we all do), but you must remember to use it to assist others in need as well. Whatever you become passionate about, use your money to further the cause for the good of humanity. Know that we are all meant to have all that is good and positive for us in this life and money can be used to attain these things. But know that money is not the source of

True happiness. It can help to bring happiness to a family who has no income or home, or to a village of people that need clean water or indoor plumbing. It can be used to feed a child or family. It can be used to build schools or help inner-city programs that need a building, computers or books to help your young people get off the streets by giving them a safe place to dream and grow. Money can be used for so many good things. When you are blessed with it, enjoy it, use it wisely. Do not hoard it and always give willingly. Learn how to multiply it the right way, whether you start a business, buy some property, help a small entrepreneur, invest in a joint venture, buy land or create a new invention etc., just make good intentions and be fair in all of your business dealings. My dearest daughter, whatever you give, you will receive back so many more times more and plus it feels really good when you give.

My Dearest Daughter,

You are Beautiful inside and out. Your beauty is a reflection of all that is good, all that is positive and strong on the inside. My dearest daughter, remember to love yourself. Remember to always ask that others see Him inside of you, which will always reflect Beauty on the outside. Remember to never be vain or arrogant because of your beauty. Know that once you become vain, your beauty disappears.

My Dearest Daughter,

If you are ever blessed to have children, know that they are the most precious gifts from God that you can receive, true miracles. They are to be loved, cherished, protected, nurtured, encouraged (Don't be a Dream Killer be a Dream Builder). Your children will adjust your life and sometimes save it (you saved mine).

They can be obedient or misbehave but always remember that they too are a human being with a mind, feelings, and wants. Just because they are younger than you, respect them and their opinions (of course making sure that their tone and words are expressed in a respectful manner). Remember to listen with a compassionate and forgiving ear and heart. Each child is different, learns and acts differently.

Recognize their individual gifts and talents and plant the appropriate seeds. Water the seeds, give them plenty of love, hugs and kisses-even when they protest. Tell them that you appreciate them and that you are proud of them, " say you are doing a great job". And even though they came from you, they are not you. It is your job to help them to become who they are in life. (I love you).

My Dearest Daughter, (I chose your beautiful name when I was nine years old. I knew as soon as I heard your name, I would one day in the future call you......). I wanted you to know that I have been honored and humbled to be your Mom. You have been such a blessing and it has been such a joy to watch you grow into this most amazing, intelligent, and beautiful young woman. I have never loved anyone as much as I have loved you. I know that all of your dreams will come true and that you will leave this Earth a much more beautiful place. I pray for you with Love. Know that our spirits will meet again.........

Love without Limits

Give Generously

Forgive Quickly

Laugh Loudly

Smile Broadly

Be Grateful

Stay Humble

Fear Nothing

Grow Continuously

Learn with Thirst

Think BIG

Dance Regularly

Let Your Thoughts Flow like Water

Give your Best in Everything

Seek Peace and Happiness Within

Live Every Day as your Last

PRAY Dutifully

With Love,

Mom

Made in the USA
Monee, IL
21 July 2020